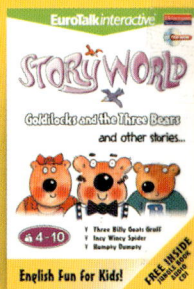

GW01452663

www.eurotalk.co.uk

learn afrikaans · learn albanian · learn american english · learn amharic · learn arabic · learn assamese · learn basque · learn bengali · learn bulgarian · learn cantonese · learn catalan · learn czech · learn danish · learn dutch · learn english · learn estonian · learn farsi · learn finnish · learn french · learn german · learn greek · learn gujarati · learn hebrew · learn hindi · learn hungarian · learn icelandic · learn igbo

70 languages! do they do Estonian?

'This is an excitingly different language learning series. Talk Now! uses games and quizzes as a basis for making the learning process fun and relaxing. There's no better way to teach an old dog new tricks and this fun element of the program means that your fears are forgotten as you absorb words and phrases without even realising you are learning them.'

PC Answers

learn zulu
learn yoruba
learn xhosa
learn welsh
learn vietnamese
learn urdu
learn ukrainian
learn turkish
learn tibetan
learn thai
learn telugu
learn tamil
learn tagalog
learn swedish

LEVEL 1 BEGINNERS
CD-ROMs for Windows® & Mac®

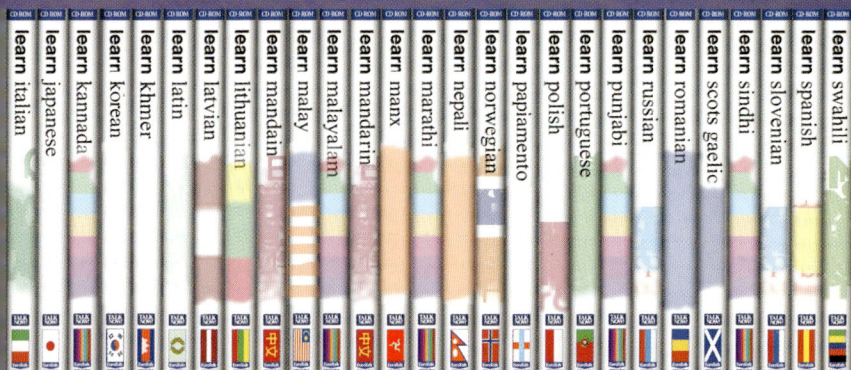

learn italian
learn japanese
learn kannada
learn korean
learn khmer
learn latin
learn latvian
learn lithuanian
learn mandarin
learn malay
learn malayalam
learn mandarin
learn manx
learn marathi
learn nepali
learn norwegian
learn papiamento
learn polish
learn portuguese
learn punjabi
learn russian
learn romanian
learn scots gaelic
learn sindhi
learn slovenian
learn spanish
learn swahili

"World Talk is the next step up [from Talk Now!], dealing with more intermediate subject matter. It's more fun and offers more features than a language tape... by the time you've mastered the content of World Talk, you'll be on the way to proficiency."

PC Direct

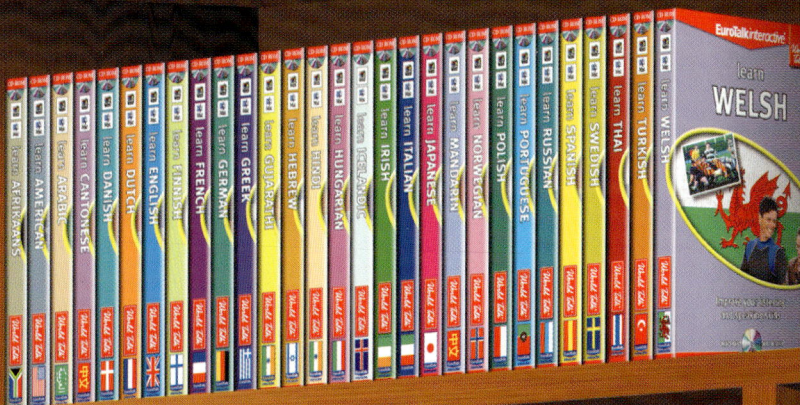

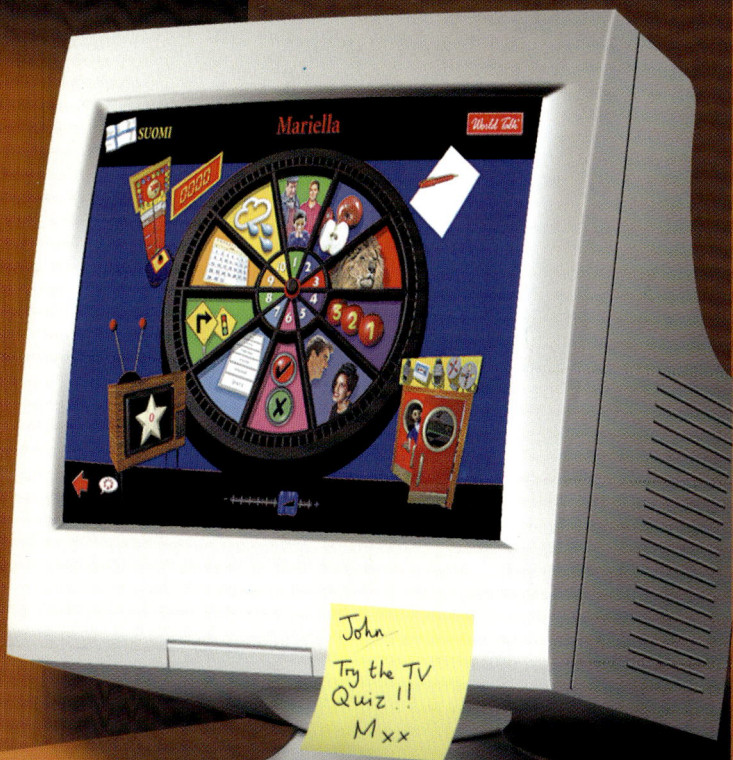

Advanced Language on DVD-R

Thanks to DVD technology, you can take part in a hugely popular film and learn a foreign language as it's really spoken.

Special features include:

- replacing your favourite character's voice with yours as the movie rolls

- playing a virtual reality game show against an on-screen competitor to test your knowledge of the film – and the language

- discovering new games and visual tricks hidden in the programme

EuroTalk interactive

Advanced
English

Interactive video language learning with
Inspector Morse "The Sins Of The Fathers"

APPLE MACINTOSH®

DVD ROM

Over 5 billion people speak langu

Asia

1. Arabic
2. Assamese
3. Bengali
4. Cantonese
5. Farsi
6. Gujarati
7. Hebrew
8. Hindi
9. Indonesian
10. Japanese
11. Kannada
12. Khmer
13. Korean
14. Malay
15. Malayalam
16. Mandarin
17. Marathi
18. Nepali
19. Punjabi
20. Russian
21. Sindhi
22. Tamil

23. Tagalog
24. Telugu
25. Thai
26. Tibetan
27. Turkish
28. Urdu
29. Vietnamese

Africa

1. Arabic
2. Afrikaans
3. Amharic
4. French
5. English
6. Igbo

7. Portuguese
8. Swahili
9. Xhosa
10. Yoruba
11. Zulu

ges taught by EuroTalk

Europe

1. Albanian
2. Basque
3. Bulgarian
4. Catalan
5. Croatian
6. Czech
7. Danish
8. Dutch
9. English
10. Estonian
11. Finnish
12. French
13. German
14. Greek
15. Hungarian
16. Icelandic
17. Irish
18. Italian
19. Latin
20. Latvian
21. Lithuanian
22. Maltese
23. Manx
24. Norwegian
25. Polish
26. Portuguese
27. Romanian
28. Russian
29. Scots Gaelic
30. Slovenian
31. Spanish
32. Swedish
33. Turkish
34. Ukrainian
35. Welsh

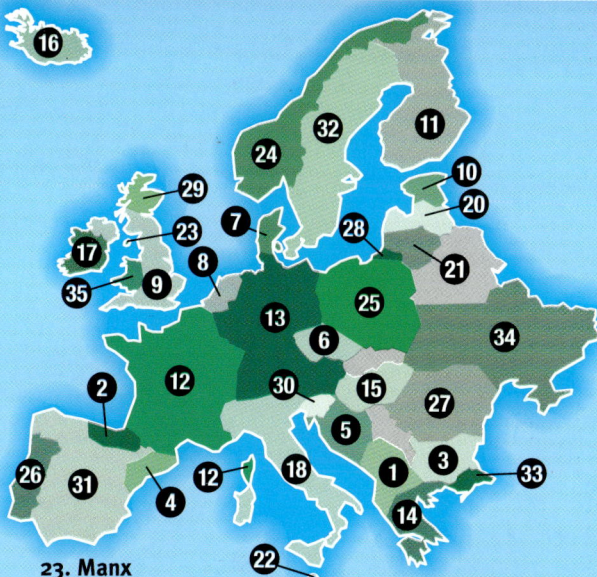

America

1. American English
2. Danish
3. Dutch
4. English
5. French
6. Papiamento
7. Portuguese
8. Spanish

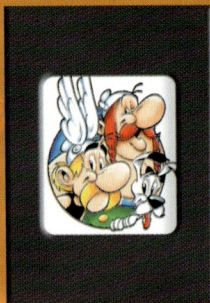

EuroTalk_interactive_

Astérix

Learn
SPANISH

2 CD ROMs

EuroTalk
interactive
Astérix
Learn
ENGLISH
2 CD-ROMS

EuroTalk
interactive
Astérix
Learn
FRENCH
2 CD-ROMS

EuroTalk
interactive
Astérix
Learn
GERMAN
2 CD-ROMS

EuroTalk
interactive
Astérix
Learn
ITALIAN

EuroTalk
interactive
Astérix
Learn
LATIN

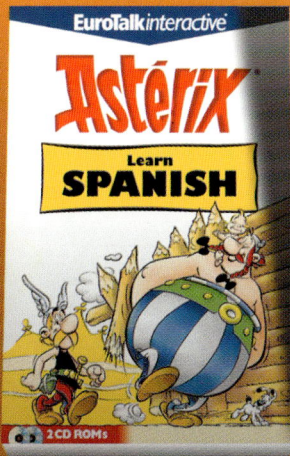

Join Asterix, Obelix, Idefix and friends in this action-packed cartoon strip. You can watch the adventure unfold, record yourself speaking the part of your favourite character and test your language skills with an interactive quiz.

"It is a highly polished product…[Asterix]…could almost be described as 'cult software'."

Computer Shopper

Vocabulary Builder

Albanian · American · Arabic · Cantonese · Chinese · Danish · Dutch · English · Finnish · French · German · Greek · Hebrew · Hungarian · Icelandic · Irish · Italian · Japanese · Norwegian · Papiamento · Polish · Portuguese · Russian · Scots Gaelic · Spanish · Swedish · Turkish

'Normal Flashcards could be boring for kids until EuroTalk, based in London came up with this innovative multimedia format for 3 – 10 year olds.... The result is a very slick disc, designed to teach vocabulary to children who have absolutely no knowledge of a foreign tongue.'

The Guardian Education

EuroTalk interactive
Vocabulary Builder
Spanish

· LANGUAGES FOR EVERYONE · LANGUAGES FOR EVERYONE ·

Story World

Using children's playtime to learn English...

CD-ROMs for Windows® & Mac®

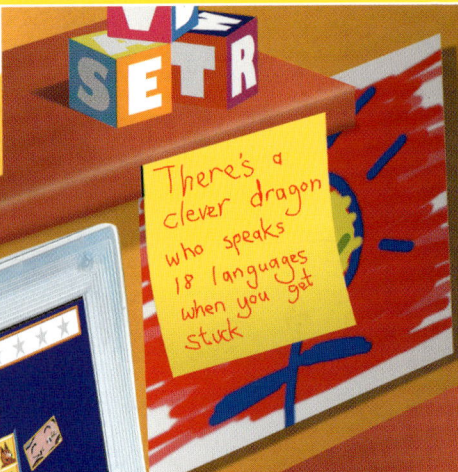

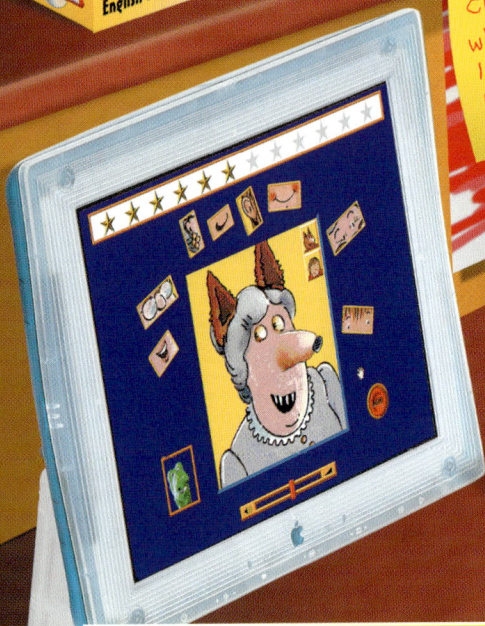

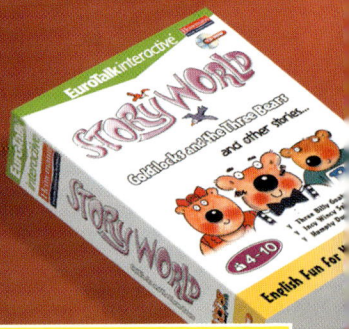

There's a clever dragon who speaks 18 languages when you get stuck

Children from 4 to 10-years-old will pester you to let them play with these – they won't even realise they're helping their language skills into the bargain.

Each disc includes four favourite children's stories which youngsters can listen to as the animated action unfolds.

But there's much more. You can record yourself narrating the story on screen – then play it back.

You can also play games including spotting the different animals in a meadow, painting the teddy bear different colours and telling the time – all in a foreign language!

Listen/Ecoutez Bien

Classroom-style lessons made fun!

CD-ROMs for Windows® & Mac®

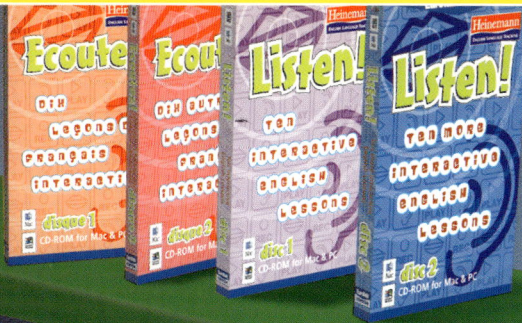

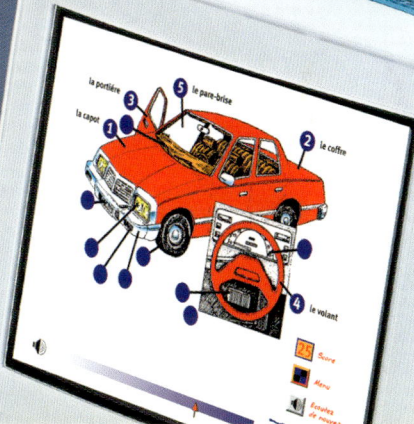

Listen/Ecoutez Bien brings traditional English or French language lessons to life for teenagers and adults.

Each disc helps you learn all the usual words you would be given in a classroom.

But instead of having to memorise them from a list, it challenges you to learn by being asked questions about them in a foreign language.

By recording your voice it perfects your accent and by asking questions it tests your understanding. Could you get full marks? Each disc covers ten fully illustrated topics.

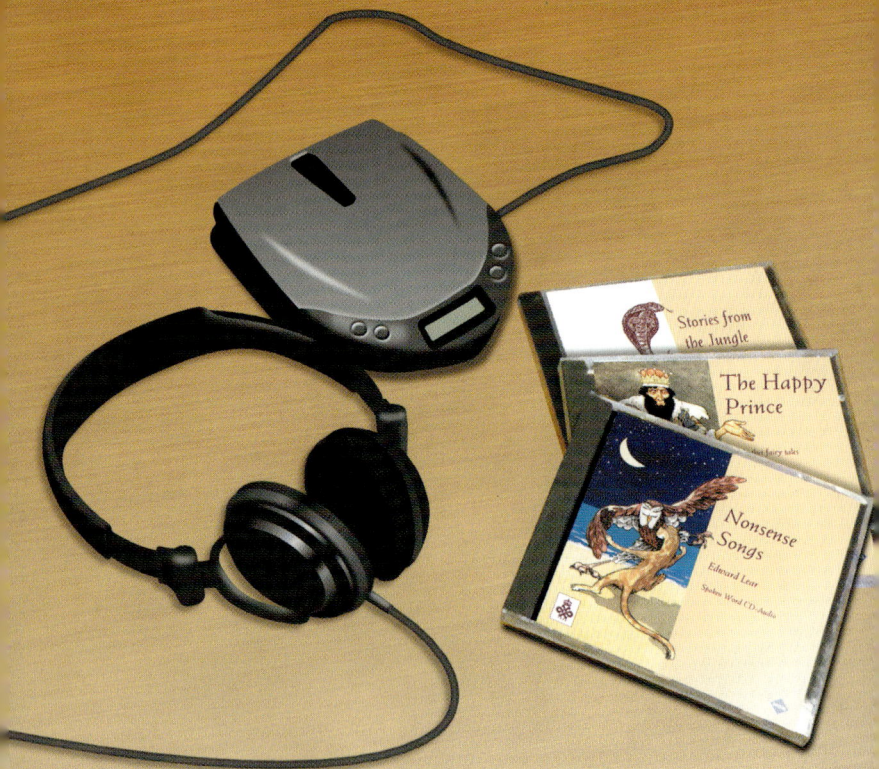

TV and radio stars, including Felicity Kendall, Robert Powell and Sarah Miles, read world-famous literary classics. Choose from:

Rudyard Kipling's "Stories from the Jungle Book"

Kipling's "Just So Stories"

Oscar Wilde's "The Happy Prince" and other stories

Hans Christian Andersen's "The Ugly Duckling" and other stories

Edward Lear's "Nonsense Songs"

Katherine Mansfield's "Bliss" and other stories

How To Order

Try your usual EuroTalk retailer particularly if you are looking for special offers or want it NOW!

Alternatively you may want to order direct from EuroTalk - we have over 150 different CD's in stock:

Visit our website **www.eurotalk.co.uk** and place your order through our secure server.

or Telephone   **0800 018 8838** (UK callers only)
                      +44 20 7371 0999 (Overseas callers)
or Fax   **+44 20 7371 7781**
or Write   **Eurotalk, 315-317 New Kings Road, London, SW6 4RF.**
                      (Cheques should be made payable to EuroTalk Interactive)

We believe in our products! If having tried one, you are not happy with it for any reason you may return it to us for a full refund.

Latest News

We are always expanding the EuroTalk range. For the latest news on what's currently available, and full product details, visit the EuroTalk website at **www.eurotalk.co.uk**. You can also email **info@eurotalk.co.uk** if you're interested in a particular language – we will then e-mail you in advance of new releases. Similarly your comments and suggestions are always welcomed.

Education

Our language learning software is ideal for use in schools and colleges and has proved particularly popular with students of all ages. The World Talk and DVD series have both won Gold PIN awards for education.

All of the products are **specifically designed to build confidence in listening and speaking skills** and support the following UK National Curriculum elements:

Talk Now – Key stages 2-3   World Talk – Key stages 3-4
Asterix – Post GCSE   Vocabulary Builder – Key stage 1 and above

Student records are a standard feature on all products and **special network versions are available**.

Licences

All EuroTalk discs are licensed for HOME USE ONLY. For details of how to obtain educational, learning centre, library and corporate licences please contact info@eurotalk.co.uk or Telephone +44 (0)20 7371 7711 or Fax +44 (0)20 7371 7781.

EuroTalk *interactive* ®

We believe there is no such thing as someone who is bad at languages – only someone who hasn't yet discovered the right way to learn.

WOOF!

...everybody should learn another language

WHAT THE PAPERS SAY

"....you'll find you just can't drag yourself away — in short, you can't stop yourself learning."
What PC? magazine

"...the most entertaining CD-ROM language packages come from the publisher EuroTalk ..."
South China Post

"...succeeds in both the entertainment and educational stakes..."
Personal Computer World

"...they are certainly addictive..."
The Times

315-317 New King's Road, Fulham, London SW6 4RF
tel: +44(0)20 7371 7711 fax: +44(0)20 7371 7781